Copyright © 2016 Luke Paulyn.

What do you call a fake noodle?

An im-pasta!

What did the spaceman say when he trod on a chocolate bar?

I just stepped on Mars!

What pie can fly?

A magpie!

What happens when it rains cats and dogs?

Try not to step in a poodle!

What do you call a rabbit dressed as a cake?

A cream bun!

What did 0 say to 8?

Nice belt!

Where did the sheep go on vacation?

The baaaahamas!

What do you call a cross between a wizard and a UFO?

A flying sorcerer!

How do you make 7 even?

Take away the 'S'!

What is a cat's favourite movie?

The sound of Mew-sic!

Why couldn't the pirate play cards?

He was sitting on the deck!

What does a brain do when it sees a friend?

Gives it a brain wave!

What does a snail say when riding on a turtle's back?

WEEEEEE!

Waiter this soup tastes funny!

Why aren't you laughing?

Why are ghosts bad liars?

You can see straight through them!

What do aliens like to read?

Comet books!

Why did the boy bring a ladder to school?

Because he was in high school!

What did the alien say to the garden?

Take me to your weeder!

Why was everyone tired on April 1st?

They had just finished a 31-day March!

What is a mouse like after a shower?

Squeaky clean!

What's the difference between a guitar and a fish?

You can't tuna fish!

What did the traffic light say to the car?

Don't look I'm changing!

What do you call a man whose dad was a canon?

A son of a gun!

What do you call a chocolate that teases animals?

A mole-teaser!

Why was the broom late?

It over-swept!

What dog can jump higher than a building?

Any dog because buildings can't jump!

Where did the king keep his armies?

Up his sleevies!

Where do wasps go when they're ill?

The waspital!

What do mermaids have on toast?

Mermerlade!

What is a pigs favourite ballet?

Swine lake!

Why was 6 afraid of 7?

Because 7 ate 9!

What instrument is in the bathroom?

A tuba toothpaste!

What has 4 legs but can't walk?

A chair!

What do you call a cow that cuts grass?

A lawnmooooooer!

What do you call a lot of birds that fly in a formation?

The Red Sparrows!

What do you call a greedy ant?

An anteater!

How does Batman's mother call him for dinner?

Dinner, dinner, dinner, dinner, Batman!

What time do people go to the dentist?

At tooth-hurty!

Where do fish keep their money?

A river-bank!

Where do pencils go on holiday?

Pencil-vania!

Where do cows go for entertainment?

The moo-vies!

What has 4 wheels and flies?

A garbage truck

Why did the child bring a ruler to bed?

He wanted to measure how long he slept!

When is it bad luck to see a black cat?

If you're a mouse!

What do you call a deer with no eyes?

No eye deer!

What do you call the owner of a chair factory?

The vice chairman!

What do you call cheese that isn't yours?

Nacho cheese!

What do you call a magical secret agent?

James Wand!

What do you call a bear with no teeth?

A gummy bear!

Why is the desert lion everyone's favourite at Christmas?

He has sandy claws!

What did the big chimney say to the little chimney?

You're too young to smoke!

Why was the cookie sad?

Because his mum was a wafer for so long!

Where does a rabbit learn to fly?

The hare force!

What did one toilet say to the other?

You look a bit flushed!

How did the barber win the race?

He knew a shortcut!

Why did the house go to the doctors?

It had window panes!

What is the strongest animal?

A snail because it carries its house on it's back!

How do you make a tissue dance?

You put a little boogie in it!

What part of a football pitch smells the nicest?

The scenter spot!

Why do athletes never sweat?

Because of all their fans!

What do you call a pig that knows karate?

A pork chop!

Why did a boy bring a pencil to bed?

So he could draw the curtains!

How do prawns and clams communicate?

With shell-phones!

Why are teddy bears never hungry?

They are always stuffed!

What do footballers and magicians have in common?

They both do hat tricks!

What do bunnies like to play?

Hop scotch!

What do you call a fly without wings?

A walk!

Why was the skeleton laughing?

Because of its funny bone!

What do you call James Bond in the bath?

Bubble 07!

How do oceans say hello?

They wave!

What do you call a car on a leash?

A carpet!

What fur do we get from a tiger?

As fur away as possible!

What did the maths book say to the other maths book?

I'm full of problems!

Why did the child study in the aeroplane?

He wanted a higher education!

Why did mickey mouse go to outer space?

He wanted to see pluto!

Why did the vampire brush its teeth?

So it didn't get bad breath!

What do you call an exploding monkey?

A baboom!

Why did the chicken cross the playground?

To get to the other slide!

If you want a fly to go away what do you say?

Buzz off!

What does a short sighted monster wear?

Spooktacles!

Why don't oysters share their pearls?

They are shellfish!

What did the policeman say to his stomach?

You're under a vest!

What did the blanket say to the bed?

Don't worry, I've got you covered!

What animal should you never play cards with?

A cheetah!

What does an elf learn in school?

The elfabet!

What day do fish hate?

Fry-day!

What do you get from a pampered cow?

Spoiled milk!

When do ghosts all trick each other?

April ghouls day!

What do you call a cross between a snowman and a vampire?

A frostbite!

How do fish get around?

On an octo-bus!

Why did the computer go to the doctor?

It had a virus!

What do you call a monster that you can only see at night?

A lampire!

What do you call a dog that likes baths?

A shampoodle!

What goes Oh! Oh! Oh!?

Backwards santa!

Why don't you do homework in the jungle?

Because if you do 4+4 you get ate!

Why do bicycles fall over?

Because they're two-tired!

Why are footballers never asked for dinner?

Because they're always dribbling!

What animal wears a wig?

A bald eagle!

What did one eye say to the other?

Something smells between us!

When do ducks wake up?

The quack of dawn!

Why does a giraffe have such a long neck?

Because its feet stink!

Who is santa's most famous elf?

Elfvis!

Where do bees wait if they need to go shopping?

The buzz-stop!

Have you heard the story of the germ?

Don't worry it will just spread!

What gets wetter the more it dries?

A towel!

What bird can you write with?

A PENguin!

Why did the oreo go to the dentist?

It lost its filling!

Why did a bald guy put a rabbit on his head?

He needed hare!

What is as big as a dinosaur but weighs nothing?

A dinosaurs shadow!

What was the pirate movie rated?

ARRRgh!

What is smaller than an ants dinner?

Its mouth!

What did the monkey say to his little brother?

You're driving me bananas!

What is brown and sticky?

A stick!

What do you call a dinosaur that never gives up?

A try and try and try-ceratops!

Which dinosaur knew the most words?

The thesaurus!

What are 2 banana peels called together?

Slippers!

What is the fastest vegetable?

A runner bean!

Which subject is the witch good at in school?

Spelling!

What do you find in a clean nose?

Finger prints!

What does a snowman eat for breakfast?

Snowflakes!

What do you call a dinosaur that never has a bath?

A stink-o-saurus!

Where do sharks come from?

Fin-land!

What do you call a messy hippo?

A hippopota-mess!

Why do fish live in salt water?

Pepper makes them sneeze!

Why did the cookie go to the doctor?

Because it felt crummy!

What did the lightning bolt say to the other lightning bolt?

You're shocking!

Why did the banana go to the doctor?

It wasn't peeling well!

What does a piece of toast wear to bed?

His PY-JAM-as!

What do you call a blind dinosaur?

A doyouthinkhesawus!

Were you long in hospital?

No, I'm the right size now!

What do you call a boomerang that doesn't come back?

A stick!

What's orange and sounds like a parrot?

A carrot!

Why was a man running around his bed?

He wanted to catch up on his sleep!

Why can't a nose be 12 inches long?

Because then it would be a foot!

What's different between a horse and the weather?

One is reined up and the other rains down!

What is the strongest vegetable?

A muscle sprout!

Where do cows go on holiday?

Moo York!

Where do orcas hear music?

Orca-stras!

Why did the orange lose the race?

He ran out of juice!

Why was the chicken afraid of the chicken?

Because it was a chicken!

Why did the skeleton not watch the scary movie?

He didn't have the guts!

What do you call a french person in the toilet?

Your-a-pee-in!

What do cows read on the toilet?

A moooospaper!

Why did the cow cross the road?

To get to the udder side!

Printed in Great Britain
by Amazon